*NSYNC

THE OFFICIAL BOOK

This book is dedicated to the family of people who made 'N Sync possible. Without their love, support, and guidance, we wouldn't be who we are today.

Especially to our fans . . . Without you none of this would be possible . . . Stay 'N Sync.

Published by
Bantam Doubleday Dell Books for Young Readers
a division of
Bantam Doubleday Dell Publishing Group, Inc.
1540 Broadway
New York, New York 10036

Book design by Ericka Meltzer O'Rourke

For my mother, Catherine A. Squires, with love
—K.M.S.

Acknowledgments:
The author wishes to thank the following people for their support and invaluable contributions to this book: Beverly Horowitz, Lawrence David, Andrew Smith, and everyone at BDD; Kaja Gula and everyone at RCA Records; as always, Ronnie Rodriguez; and especially the guys and their families for their cooperation: JC, Lance, Joey, Justin, and Chris—I had a great time getting to know you.—K.M.S.

Visit us on the Web! www.bdd.com
Educators and librarians, visit the BDD Teacher's Resource Center at www.bdd.com/teachers

ISBN: 0-440-41636-1
Printed in the United States of America
December 1998
10 9 8 7

Five 'Ncredible Guys

THEY SNAGGED A RECORD DEAL, struck gold, and embarked on a sold-out European tour just a little over a year after their formation. Four months after its release in the United States, their debut album, *'N Sync,* raced up to the *Billboard* top ten and hit platinum.

Thousands of fan letters pour in from all over the world every day. Ardent admirers mob them wherever they go. But if you ask them, the five talented hunks behind the pop sensation 'N Sync say they're just a bunch of regular guys.

Regular guys who can blend vocal harmonies to perfection. Ordinary Joes whose moves rival Michael Jackson's. Guys next door who just happen to be taking the music world by storm.

But the truth is, offstage, these five amazing talents *do* seem like everyday guys. Spending time with this gifted but easygoing bunch is like hanging out with lifelong neighborhood pals.

Who are these 'Ncredible guys? They are: James "Lansten" Lance Bass, 19, laid-back, soft-spoken animal lover; suave, blue-eyed Joshua Scott "JC" Chasez, 22,; Joseph "Joey" Anthony Fatone, Jr., 21, a fun-loving, easygoing kid at heart; Christopher "Chris" Alan Kirkpatrick, 27, tattooed and dreadlocked; and Justin Randall Timberlake, 17, with his distinctive, soulful voice.

Clean, mellow harmonies and toe-tapping grooves set 'N Sync apart from anyone else on the pop charts today. Their repertoire ranges from infectious dance tunes and smooth, easy ballads to amazing a cappella melodies and freshly reworked covers. But it's their live shows that attract the most attention. 'N Sync's high-energy concerts feature incredible vocals, expertly choreographed dance routines, awesome acrobatics, and an abundance of audience interaction.

Mostly, it's their authenticity that shines. In this all-'Nclusive biography of the pop sensation, you'll get to know the men behind the music. You'll hear in their own words how they came together. You'll learn their likes and dislikes, what they look for in a girl, and what their parents think of their success. You'll discover how 'N Sync makes its own brand of musical magic. It's all here.

Together as a group for only four weeks: 'N Sync in New York City in November 1995.
(Photograph courtesy of the Bass family)

'N the Beginning

THERE ARE A TON OF BOY BANDS on the charts today, all competing for the top spots. What makes 'N Sync so special?

'N Sync stands out because the young men in it are genuine; they're not a prepackaged rent-a-band put together by big-time music promoters. Justin Timberlake explains: "We put the group together ourselves. I think that's something that's paid off in the long run because we were friends before we got a management team and before we got a record deal."

Lance Bass agrees. "Everything that we do is always together, and I think that's what makes the group unique."

The web of their friendship is dizzying. Flashback to 1995: Pennsylvania native Chris Kirkpatrick was living in Orlando, Florida, and working at Universal Studios as a doo-wop singer. It was there that he met and became friendly with Brooklyn-born Joey Fatone. Meanwhile, Washington, D.C., native JC Chasez and Memphis boy Justin Timberlake had just wrapped a stint together on *The Mickey Mouse Club,*

The group in Warsaw, Poland, on its 1996 European Tour. (Photograph courtesy of the Bass family)

also in Orlando. Justin knew Chris from auditions, and JC was friendly with Joey, whose high-school buddies had also been on *The Mickey Mouse Club*.

Chris was itching to put a group together—a group who could take five-part harmonies and translate them into pop music. He contacted Justin, who, he knew, could sing. Justin enlisted JC, and soon old pal Joey fell into the fold.

The foursome was ready to make a go of it, but they lacked something important. Though Chris, JC, Justin, and Joey had wide vocal ranges, not one of them felt he had a solid enough bass.

Justin immediately called his vocal coach back home in Memphis, hoping the coach would be able to recommend the perfect "low guy." Enter James "Lansten" Lance Bass, a good-natured country boy from Clinton, Mississippi. Lance jumped on the next flight to Orlando and, upon arrival, instantly hit it off with the guys. Chris, Justin, Joey, and JC knew they had found their final member.

'N Sync with its first gold CD. (Photograph courtesy of the Fatone family)

Now all they needed was a name. They brainstormed for weeks, but nothing seemed right; nothing seemed to fit these five fab fellows and their unique sound. Until, one day, Justin's mom remarked how "in sync" their harmonies and dancing were. The phrase stuck with the guys. "In Sync" had a nice ring to it.

But Justin's mom wasn't sure that the guys were convinced. Going back to the drawing board, she started playing around with their initials. She got nothing but gobbledygook out of the initials of their first and last names, so she started to toy with the last letters of their first names. After some shifting and scrambling, she came up with Justi**N**, Chri**S**, Joe**Y**, Lanste**N**, and J**C**. It was too eerie a coincidence. These guys *were* completely 'N Sync. The name 'N Sync perfectly summed up everything about the band. Five guys with five diverse backgrounds, from five different parts of the United States, with various musical influences, somehow managed to make a sound that worked.

Though all the guys cite current hot musicians like Boys II Men and Brian McKnight as vocal influences, each of them brings his personal taste to the mix. Joey claims fifties and sixties groups such as Frankie Lymon and the Teenagers and the Temptations as a huge influence; Lance offers a country twang and a love of Garth Brooks; Chris patterns his moves and high soprano after Michael Jackson; JC contributes a love of jazz and Sting's smoky vocal style; and Justin throws in a little bit of Stevie Wonder's soul with hip-hop energy.

Chris describes 'N Sync's combined sound as "purely original. It's pop, with an R&B twist. We take a lot of up-tempo songs and put harmonies behind them." Once they had their sound down, the guys were pumped up and ready to board the bullet train to success. They took every gig they could get, from coffeehouses to discos to theme parks.

Shortly after forming as a group in 1995, they cut a video demo. Justin remembers, "We did our demo package as fast as we could, and that's when we got in touch with our management." Chris recalls the demo with a tinge of embarrassment. "It was very, very rough. We did it last-minute, but it was all done by us—the printing of the posters, the choosing of the outfits, the song orders, the choreography—everything. It was a lot of work." The demo included a few originals and one cover: a funky version of the Beatles' classic "We Can Work It Out."

In 1996, a year after 'N Sync formed, the demo captured the eye and ear of Lou Pearlman, the band's current business manager. Lou immediately got in touch with Johnny Wright, the mastermind manager behind such hit groups as New Kids on the Block, Snap, Color Me Badd, and the Backstreet Boys.

Johnny recollects what made him sit up and take notice of this particular gang of five: "They could really sing. They had a chemistry—an aura about them. When they talked to me they talked to me as a group, as a unit, rather than five individuals trying to pitch themselves to me—they weren't selfish. They had the same kind of aura [as New Kids on the Block]," he says fondly. "They came across my partner, Lou Pearlman. I was in Germany, and Lou called me one night and said, 'Hey, you'll never believe what's in Orlando. Another great bunch of guys. You've got to come check them out!' So I checked them out and agreed. We had the perfect opportunity to land a record deal for them. The stars were lined up for them."

Wright had no problem obtaining a record contract at BMG in Germany for 'N Sync. "He hooked us up with our record company," Justin says, "and Lou Pearlman, our business manager, was also good friends with the record company. The whole team hooked us up with BMG, and they took us to Europe. We were, like, we don't care where you take us—we just want to sing!"

Power producers Denniz Pop and Max Martin, who worked with international superstars Ace of Base and Robyn, were the next to join the team. The first single, and first smash hit, "I Want You Back," came out of the collaboration. In a few months' time, 'N Sync had a gold record on its hands.

Immediately, almost miraculously, the band broke long-standing European records, knocking out Michael Jackson as the king of the quickest-rising single and capturing the

The guys in Switzerland, 1996. (Photograph courtesy of the Bass family)

title for longest reign for a new act on the charts. "Tearin' Up My Heart" followed quickly on the first single's heels, debuting in the top five. When 'N Sync's album was finally finished, it soared to number one faster than you can say "overnight sensation." Suddenly the guys of 'N Sync were pursued by frenzied fans wherever they went.

A sold-out tour followed, bringing them not only across the European continent but to the United Kingdom, Mexico, South Africa, Asia—everywhere but home, sweet home, the U.S.A. But success in the guys' own country wasn't too far off. After establishing a foothold in the European market, 'N Sync was ready to come home.

Two years later in 1998, when the group returned to the States, there were no swarms of fans waiting in every corner. Chris considered it a "reality check," and he actually relished going to the movies or eating at a restaurant as a face in the crowd.

He had no idea what they were in for.

When *'N Sync* hit the stores in April 1998, the singles "I Want You Back" and "Tearin' Up My Heart" were already picking up steam. But the boys never expected that the album would go platinum within four months of its release. Abruptly, anonymity was something they couldn't have at home any longer.

They started their first U.S. tour after the release of the album, and along with their newfound fame came crowds—and opportunities. Numerous television appearances followed. They filmed a Disney concert special, performed at the Miss Teen USA pageant, and made guest appearances on *The Tonight Show, Live with Regis and Kathie Lee,* and MTV.

With the grueling schedule and extraordinary demands on their time, it's amazing that the quintet didn't burn out after the first year. And if they didn't get sick of the routine, certainly they must have been ready to run from each other!

Not true, each and every guy confirms. "When we get time off there won't be a day that goes by that I don't talk to one of them and say what are you doing tonight, do you want to go do something?" Justin says.

JC agrees. "There's nothing better than going out with your friends and having a good time. And that's what it is. These guys are my best friends, and we get to go out and we get to see each other have fun. That's the best part about the job."

'N Sync certainly exceeded all expectations by pursuing the simple dream of getting together and having a good time. The five may have taken the world by storm awfully quickly, but it seems their fame will last a lot longer than the requisite fifteen minutes. Just ask their fans.

Joseph "Joey" Anthony Fatone, Jr.: Happy-Go-Lucky Heartthrob

Birth date: January 28, 1977

Place of birth: Brooklyn, New York

Eyes: Brown

Hair: Brown

Home: Orlando, Florida

Family: Mother, Phyllis; father, Joe senior.; sister, Janine, 26; brother, Steven, 23

Favorite food: Italian

Car: Acura SLX

Star sign: Aquarius

Best mates: Libra, Sagittarius, Aries, Gemini

Favorite film star: Robert De Niro

Favorite colors: Purple and red

Favorite music: Musicals and movie soundtracks

Collector's item: Superman memorabilia

Favorite childhood toy, according to Mom: "It was a red, white, and blue monkey, but he doesn't have it anymore. He loved hand puppets. He still has one, a big brown monkey that his aunt bought him that still sits in his room."

Favorite 'N Sync song: "'I Want You Back' because it was the first to go gold."

Top: Baby Joey.
Bottom: Joey in preschool.
(Photographs courtesy of the Fatone family)

YOU'D NEVER BELIEVE THAT smooth-moving Joey Fatone used to be a klutz, but according to his parents, he was incredibly accident-prone up until the age of five. "The emergency room staff knew him by his first name," his father, Joe senior, says, laughing.

"Before he was five years old, he had about twelve stitches and eighteen butterflies," adds Joey's mom, Phyllis. "He always had a cape on, and he used to [try to] fly through the windows like Superman! He had stitches from head to toe, and now he has scars all over. After age five, from then on he became a showster. He loved to pretend, with his cousins and brother and sister. They would always get together and put shows on."

Joey grew up in Brooklyn, New York, surrounded by music and theater. He credits his father, who sang in a little-known doo-wop band and ran a theater group, with developing his love of music. "He was always surrounded by music and bands," Joey's mom confirms. "Fifties and sixties music. [His father's group] would sing right in our house, with the speakers and everything, and the kids would sit there with their mouths open, watching everything they did."

Joey claims that the fifties and sixties groups his father introduced him to, such as Frankie Lymon and the Teenagers and the Temptations, in addition to modern vocalists Boys II Men, greatly influenced his

current singing style. But it wasn't just music that cultivated a love of the spotlight in young Joey. Once Joe senior saw that his kids had talent and an interest in performing, he put young Joey and his siblings in his shows.

"We used to belong to three or four different churches that had theater guilds," Phyllis recalls, "and the kids were always there, always onstage." She fondly remembers Joey's first stage performance, in *Oklahoma!* The first song she remembers him singing? "Tequila," complete with his own dance routine.

Joey remembers the first time he felt that performing was what he wanted to do. "It was when I was in kindergarten or first grade. It was a family-theater type of thing. I played a little part in a scene from *Pinocchio,*" he says. "From that moment on, it looked like a lot of fun. I thought it was the greatest feeling to get applause—to get to feed off the audience. I loved being onstage and watching people's faces. I still like getting that response."

When Joey was thirteen, his family moved to Orlando, which for him would be an important stepping-stone to a professional performing career. "I used to do a lot of Shakespearean plays, musicals, and one-act plays in high school. That's when I first really started doing stuff. I tried to pull in a little bit of everything—I was singing and dancing and acting."

After high school, Joey scored a singing and dancing gig at Universal Studios in *The Beetlejuice Graveyard Revue.* He calls it a "great learning experience" as well as fun. Plus he

Left: Photograph by Lawrence David, copyright © 1998 by Bantam Doubleday Dell
Right: Photograph courtesy of Kaja Gula

had his brother and sister to pal around with on the job: Both Steven and Janine Fatone also worked at Universal. But perhaps the best thing about Joey's Universal gig was meeting up with Chris Kirkpatrick. Chris's baritone-tenor voice and high falsetto proved to be the perfect addition to 'N Sync.

From the beginning, Joey threw his time and energy into the band. "We knew we were in for a lot of work," he says. "When we had no record company, no management, when we first started and we were just rehearsing, I was still working, and I would go to work during the day and rehearse at night, from nine to midnight. It took a lot of hard work, dedication, and some sacrifices. Once I found out we signed with the record label I was like, 'Okay, I have to quit my job.' It was kind of weird."

Though the whirlwind success of 'N Sync may have come as a surprise to Joey, his mother wasn't the least bit fazed. "I always knew Joey would be in the field doing something," she confides. "He was the type of kid that went at it, and he fought for it. He would do anything to follow his dreams." For her son, success is exactly what Phyllis Fatone had hoped for.

But with the staggering success came a lot of sudden changes. "I have no time on my hands anymore," Joey wistfully admits. "I [miss] family things. People take it for granted that it's an everyday thing. But Christmas and New Year's, times when you're usually with your family . . . those are some of the times you're not there. Not being able to go on dates is a hard thing too. We try to as much as we can when we have the time off."

Despite his schedule, Joey remains incredibly close to his family. He still lives in Orlando with his parents, in the same home where he spent his teenage years. "It's easier, and I don't have to pay rent!" he points out. "Plus, I'm never around."

His mother loves it when Joey does have the time to come home, but she laughingly complains, "I still have to tell him to pick up his clothes and make his bed, and not to throw his socks on the floor and to put his shoes away." With his success, she says, she needs "more closets! It's unbelievable, everything he brings home! Gifts from fans, clothes that sponsors give them, sneakers. I have a closet just full of sneakers! But he has some really nice things that fans have given him. They've knitted him sweaters . . . beautiful stuff."

Joey observes that his family is "very excited" about his success. "They try to get involved in any way they can," he says.

"They're always asking if there's anything they can do . . . the whole family is supportive. Even when I was in high school, when I was in a group with four other guys, they supported us then in whatever we did, and tried to be there whenever we performed."

Joey adds that his family still chips in. "My mom is trying to answer fan mail. But now the fan mail is starting to get more and more. She also helps with my personal financial stuff. My dad helps me make sure I'm making the right choices. He's never going to make decisions for me—he wants me to learn on my own. But he'll help me out."

Joey's mom is proud to say that the entire family "backs him up one hundred percent," and she is touched by the close contact Joey keeps with them when he is on the road. "He gets yelled at every month about his phone bills. I talk to Joey at least two to three times a day." She also appreciates that Joey "wants us there with him" as often as possible. "We go whenever we can."

Joey's family has traveled with him in the United States, Canada, Mexico, and Europe on many occasions. Everywhere, Phyllis Fatone is constantly astounded by the fans' reactions to her son, and she counts it as the best part of being the mom of a pop singer. "I enjoy seeing their enjoyment. It's very, very exciting. It's a nice feeling." But the most difficult part is watching her son "have a hard time getting around . . . going out, going to a movie." Often, she says, "he's surrounded" by fans.

Even at home in Orlando, "We have fans always coming to the door," Phyllis says with amazement. "We don't mind it. If Joey's here, he'll go out, and stand with them and take pictures. It used to be just Europeans, and now we're getting American kids from the neighborhood."

But she adds sternly, "I don't want it to go to his head. I want him to enjoy it. I want him to spend his money wisely, but to enjoy everything in life. Buy a big, beautiful home, buy the cars that he likes, but not to be a show-off. I don't want that at all, and I don't think he'll be like that. He's so good with us. He helps us with everything."

It seems that she has nothing to worry about. Joey is genuine and down-to-earth, and he maintains an optimistic outlook and cheery spirit. He describes himself as the "happy-go-lucky guy" of the group. "When people are down I try to cheer them up. I'm always happy."

It's apparent that he enjoys every part of his job, "from signing autographs, because you're meeting people who are interested in meeting you; to being onstage performing, having that front to show your music; to the recording, where you get to be creative and use ideas," he says. "Even at the photo shoots, I learn about photography . . . you always learn by watching."

But to Joey, the best thing about his job is traveling the world. "I liked Germany because of its architecture. And South Africa is just beautiful. Asia . . . they're very nice over there. Every place had its moments. I wanted to check out anything and everything that I could."

Joey is a shutterbug who carts his video camera wherever he goes. "He has footage from all over the world," bandmate JC says. Joey takes in everything about a new place and its people when he visits. "Every place is different," he says. "In Germany they're very dedicated fans; they will follow you who knows how many miles to see your show. Then you have Spain, where they try to grab any article of clothing or your face . . . anything just to touch you. All of them love the music, enjoy the music, love watching us perform. In Asia they're a little bit more quiet . . . they ask very politely, 'May I take a picture with you? Can I present you with this gift?' It's very nice they're very polite."

But as much as Joey enjoys traveling, he looks forward to his few days off, and he especially cherishes opportunities to come home and relax. When he has spare time, he likes to date. He wishes he had a steady girlfriend, but the rigors of the road make it hard for him to sustain a long-term relationship. To find a lucky girl to take out for a night on the town, Joey seeks out someone "outgoing," with "a great personality," who "maintains herself" and is "honest" and, above all, "understanding."

He adds, "A fun girl who enjoys company, can take a joke, and likes going to the movies. I like girls who aren't afraid to speak their mind. I don't really have a type.

I like women with long hair, short hair, red hair, dark hair—it doesn't matter!" His dream date consists of "going to the movies or a club." Hint, girls: He enjoys Top 40 and techno hot spots. "Just make sure to be yourself," he concludes.

Though Joey admits that he isn't the most agile sportsman, he does enjoy jet-skiing when he can. "We actually did a photo shoot one time with jet-skiing, and it was fun! I love doing it; I always try whenever I get some free time. I'm not the best at it. But I have fun just going fast and turning."

While he spends his free days as a speed demon on the water, Joey likes to spend his evenings "sleeping, going to the movies, going to clubs," or hunting down Superman memorabilia for his collection. His favorite items include a Superman necklace, a vinyl Superman record album from 1966, and a sweater that a fan knitted him that features the famous "S" logo.

Like all the guys, Joey has a realistic grasp on his fame, and he tries as much as possible to lead a regular life. His mother says the public Joey and the private Joey

Photographs courtesy of Kaja Gula

are one and the same. "He's a party kid, likes his girls, flirting since he was in kindergarten," she says. "He hasn't changed at all."

In ten years' time, Joey would like to be "still singing, maybe get back into acting." He thinks it would be fun for 'N Sync to branch out and work with other artists, like Janet Jackson or someone with a completely different sound from theirs, like Jewel.

He can't help hoping that 'N Sync will be around for years to come, and he suspects that it will be, citing the group's strong friendship and his personal philosophy as the secrets behind his success. "Always try your best," he likes to tell fans. "If there's a weak spot, try to work on it as hard as you can. Try to put all of your effort and focus into it." Whatever his secret, fans will share his wish for staying power and are sure to support fun-loving Joey Fatone in whatever his bright future may bring.

James "Lansten" Lance Bass: Laid Back and Lovin' Life

Birth date: May 4, 1979

Place of birth: Clinton, Mississippi

Eyes: Green

Hair: Blond

Home: Orlando, Florida, and Mississippi

Family: Mother, Diane; father, Jim; sister, Stacy, 22

Favorite food: French toast, Mexican

Car: None

Star sign: Taurus

Best mates: Libra, Virgo, Cancer

Favorite TV personalities: Rosie O'Donnell, Lucille Ball

Favorite film stars: Tom Hanks, Meg Ryan

Favorite colors: Vivid red, vivid blue

Favorite movies: *Armageddon, Clue*

Favorite TV shows: *Friends, I Love Lucy*

Favorite music: Brian McKnight, Garth Brooks

Collector's items: Pictures, old comic books, stamps, antique knives and guns

Favorite childhood toy, according to Mom: "A Mickey Mouse that he carried around until he was five years old. 'Mik Mouse,' as he was called, was lost for a day once and Lance cried himself to sleep. But we found him, and Mik Mouse is still around."

Favorite 'N Sync song: "'God Must Have Spent a Little More Time on You' because the words and melody are incredible. I get chill bumps whenever I listen to it."

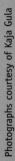

WHEN LANCE BASS WENT ON his first musical tour with a show choir that competed across the country, he never imagined that one day he'd be in a smash pop group, touring the world.

His mother, Diane, knew that Lance "secretly dreamed" of a professional singing career, but they had never seriously discussed it until he received that fateful phone call from his vocal coach asking if he'd be interested in joining up with four Orlando-based singers. "Lance has been given a gift and I accept that," his mom says. "God, no doubt, opened up these doors for him to have the opportunity, and now I cannot imagine Lance doing anything else."

She did, however, spot his talent from an early age. The first song Lance's mother remembers him singing is "Jesus Loves Me," and she laughingly recalls that he and his sister, Stacy, "were always putting on 'shows' for us. They would dress up, then make their daddy and me be the audience as they danced and sang up a storm. I also remember watching his beaming, happy face at church when the children's choir performed."

Though Diane Bass "did some singing" when she was young, she says, "Lance pretty much discovered his love for music on his own. We never really pushed it; however, music was always a part of our family entertainment."

She describes Lance as a "joy" as a child. "Kind, sweet, loving. He was always happy and tried to please everyone, including his teachers. He had so many dreams for his future. When he was around five years old he announced that he was going to be an astronaut, a movie star, president of 'the company,' *and* own a restaurant."

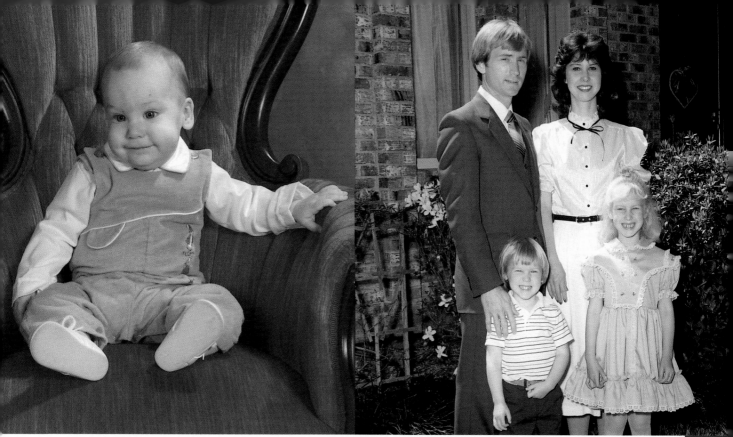

Left: Baby Lance. Right: The Bass family: Jim, Diane, Lance, and Stacy. (Photographs courtesy of the Bass family)

Lance remembers the first time he knew he wanted to perform: "The first time I knew that I wanted to be onstage was when I saw Garth Brooks in concert. I was fourteen. I thought his show was incredible. I thought, 'That's what I want to do.'"

But despite his aspirations, life before 'N Sync was pretty simple for low-key Lance. "I was just in school. The only musical thing I did was show choirs. I did that for a couple of years, eighth grade and ninth grade, and then I joined a group called Attache, which was through the school. And that was a show choir that toured around the country and competed against other ones. That was cool because it was the number-one show choir in the country. That's where I really learned how to sing and dance."

Justin's vocal coach helped him out in one of his first show choirs. "Then when Justin called him up for a bass, he recommended me," Lance recalls. He says he didn't formally audition for the group, and that he hit it off with the guys instantly. "They just flew me

down and I met them and joined that day. We sang 'The Star-Spangled Banner' together or something like that, and that was it."

From that moment on, Lance's life underwent a windstorm of change. He loves the fact that he "meets totally new people every day, gets to see the world, and shares [his] music with everybody," but he misses his privacy. "There's no privacy. I also miss hanging out with my friends and family. I hardly get to see them now."

Lance's mother agrees. "The most difficult part is not getting to see each other as much as we would like. We are such a close family and miss each other terribly." But she adds that the best part of being the parent of a singing sensation is that "we truly enjoy watching them perform. We just never seem to get enough of it."

Despite his skyrocket to the top, Lance's mom asserts that "Lance has been able to somehow keep his feet on the ground. I told Lance when he became a part of 'N Sync that the only way I would regret all this is if he changed from the good, sweet person he has always been. He hasn't lost sight of who he is and continues to hold on to the values he knows are important." She goes on, as only a mother could: "He is absolutely the sweetest person I've ever known, and always has been. The thing is that he has not changed through all of this; he is still the same person he always was. He's a very caring person, real giving, and he wants everybody to love him and he gives a lot of love . . . that's the kind of person he is. He has a real strong value system. He hangs real tight with that . . . and I'm real proud of him in that way. He's his own person and he's not easily led."

Because she knows Lance has his head on straight, Diane says she doesn't have many worries about him, except "at times I worry about his safety because they travel so much." But more than worrying, she and Lance's family pray for his well-being. "Every parent wants their child to be healthy and happy."

It seems that her prayers have been answered. Lance loves his career and the diversity it offers. "When you're through recording, you're ready to go on tour," he says. "When you're through with the tour, you're ready for a promotional tour. By the end of what you're doing, you're so ready to go on to the next thing." He adds that he never gets tired of singing and performing. "It just gets better and better," he claims, and says stepping out in front of a sea of hysterical fans is "total energy. Total adrenaline pumping. We never get scared anymore."

Lance describes his family as "very supportive. My mom [gave up teaching and] traveled with us the first year we were together." Though she officially turned him loose from the apron strings when he became eighteen in 1997, Diane appreciates Lance's daily efforts to call, no matter where he is and what he's doing. "He knows how much keeping in touch means to us, and I think it helps him, too." Now that she has gone back to teaching, Lance's mom still tries to visit him on the road. "His dad and I travel with the guys for a few days at a time whenever possible, usually around three times a year."

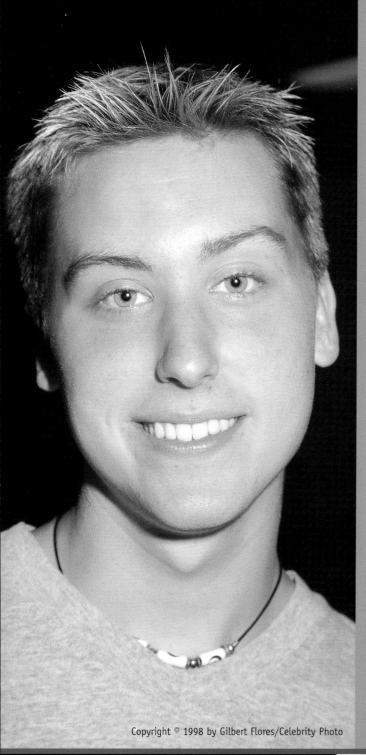

Back in her Mississippi classroom, Diane Bass has found many of her son's fans among her sixth-graders. Her students "are just real excited." And believe it or not, her 'N Sync connection has been bolstering many grades. "Every week we have a drawing for 'N Sync stuff for those who do their homework every day. Stickers, posters, things like that. Most of my students do their homework because they are so excited about that."

But even more than her students, Diane says Lance's success has affected his family. "All of his family, including grandparents, aunts, uncles, and cousins." She adds that Lance's sister is especially "proud of Lance and seems to accept the changes in our lives."

What about the screaming fans, who act as if they would do anything to get close to her son? How does she feel about his amazing popularity? "It is so hard to describe the overwhelming emotions you feel," she says. "I am so proud of him and happy for him that I sometimes feel like I will burst from joy. You

feel like laughing and crying at the same time."

Even though Lance has to leave his parents and sister behind most of the time, he feels he has four brand-new adoptive brothers. In his new "family" Lance describes himself as "the business one of the group. I like to make sure everything is going great. [I like] to try to get gigs and get to know all the business people." His bandmates agree. "When I think of Lance I think of someone toward management," Joey says. Justin adds, "Lance *is* a businessman. He's very professional."

Business-brain Lance wanted to prove a point when the boys debuted in the United States. "Over in Europe there's a big stereotype of a group like us because there's one hundred and sixty-something who try to be just like us," he explains. "But there's a big stereotype that only teenage girls go to the concerts and buy the music. That's what we wanted to eliminate. We do try to appeal to a broader market, and it's working. Over in America we don't have that stereotype. Here we have a broad market from seven years old to seventy years old. They *all* go to our concerts and buy our music."

He is quick to praise his supporters. "We love our fans," he says appreciatively. "The fans are what make us. We love spending time with them and meeting everybody, and our fans are just incredible. . . . It's good to be a part of someone's life like that. When someone recognizes you it makes you feel so good."

The offstage Lance enjoys "going to the beach, jet-skiing, trying out different places to go on vacation. I also like to go home and relax with my friends and family." He describes himself as "the all-American dude from Mississippi," whose personal style "changes day to day. Sometimes I'll go sporty, but I like to dress up a lot . . . for fancy restaurants or different parties."

He, like Joey, is not a big sports fan. He claims that he is "bad" at basketball, but he'll play with the guys because "I like to try things." How does he keep fit, then? "Doing the concerts. Our shows are so action-packed—it's a big hour-and-a-half workout every night."

His busy schedule doesn't allow him to have a girlfriend, and Lance is reluctant to say that he wishes he did. "I don't wish," he says seriously. "Because right now it's impossible to have any kind of relationship."

"I like the innocent-type girls, not too goody-goody but ones that respect themselves," he says thoughtfully. "I like a religious girl. Someone that keeps herself up and someone who could be a big supporter to me and someone who just has a good time. I also like someone who could take a joke and is fun to be with—someone adventurous like me who's willing to go parasailing and stuff . . . also someone who is loving and cute."

What kind of date could Lance's dream girl expect? "Something different. Something adventurous, like going out rock climbing, hiking, or going to the beach, having fun," he says. In fact, the beach is where Lance seems the happiest. "I love the beach," he confesses. "I'm the biggest beach bum."

As a country boy, Lance also enjoys horseback riding. "I'm from Mississippi, so there's lots of horses to choose from. I remember growing up going to camp with my church and I would always go horseback riding . . . and it was my favorite thing to do. I wanted to do it professionally, but I could never get it quite right, doing tricks and stuff."

Fans are awfully glad that Lance is a singer and not a jockey. But there are other dreams Lance would like to follow up on: He hopes to act one day, and perhaps to get into management.

Lance's mother is happy that he pictures himself as broadly involved in the entertainment business. "I just want Lance to do what fulfills him and makes his life complete," she

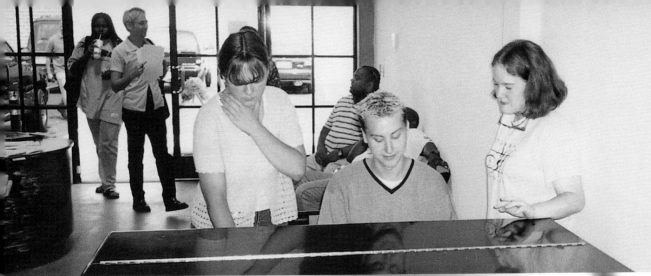
Lance plays the piano for some fans. (Photograph courtesy of Kaja Gula)

says. "[He] is interested in all aspects of the music industry, and because he is so young he has so many options in his future."

Levelheaded Lance gives his future a lot of thought. Professionally, he'd like to "win a Grammy and have the chance to meet Rosie O'Donnell and Garth Brooks" while continuing to "learn about music management." His long-term goals include "starting a family."

Lance likes to give this practical advice to his fans: "Never give up, but always have something to fall back on. [Some] people spend their whole lives trying to do something, and it's not meant for [them] . . . and I hate to see them have nothing to fall back on and make their lives into nothing."

He adds that dedication and hard work are important in anything a person chooses to do. And Lance is certainly used to working hard. His mother likes to tell this story of a much younger Lance, which resounds today: "When he was real little his daddy would pick him up from day care in the morning, and Lance would have been playing so hard, he would say, 'Hard day, Daddy, Hard day.' And I always think of that, especially when he would be so tired from being with 'N Sync all day. I would think of that little thing he would always say. I say that to him now, because I know how grueling his days are. 'Hard day, Lance. Hard day.'"

Though he's been through the hardest-working days in his young life, Lance quickly asserts, "The best days of my life, most of them have been in this group."

Christopher "Chris" Alan Kirkpatrick: Wild Man with a Dream Strikes Gold

Birth date: October 17, 1971

Place of birth: Clarion, Pennsylvania

Eyes: Brown

Hair: Brown

Home: Orlando, Florida

Family: Mother, Beverly Eustice; sisters, Molly, 24, Kate, 22, Emily, 16, and Taylor, 5

Favorite food: Tacos

Car: None

Star sign: Libra

Best mates: Gemini, Leo, Aquarius

Favorite film stars: Adam Sandler, Jackie Chan, Bruce Lee

Favorite color: Silver

Favorite music: Busta Rhymes, Beastie Boys

Favorite TV shows: *The Simpsons, South Park,* all cartoons

Collector's items: Records

Favorite childhood toy, according to Mom: "He used to collect teddies. He still has most of them. And this is funny—he had a doll that I made of leftover pieces of sheet, and he called him Joey! He dragged Joey around until Joey's head nearly fell off."

Favorite 'N Sync song: "'Giddy Up,' since we wrote it. I can remember when we were in the studio writing that and how much fun it was to write with the other guys."

WHEN CHRIS KIRKPATRICK TOLD his mother that he had an idea to put together a group of five singing and dancing young guys, she wasn't the least bit surprised. "Everyone in my family is a musician," Beverly Eustice says. "So saying that you want to put together a band in my family is a lot like telling somebody you want to learn to ride a bike in someone else's family. It's real normal. My grandparents both had bands. My mother trained in opera. My dad made five records—he was a country-western singer. My sister sings rockabilly and jazz in Pittsburgh, my brother was a rock singer, my little brother is a country singer in Nashville, my nephew has a band. I teach voice lessons but I'm actually an instrumentalist. So it's not really that extraordinary. It's what we do."

Obviously, Chris was born to follow in his family's footsteps and excel in the music field. He was always surrounded by music and from birth showed a keen talent. "Before he was talking he was making sounds, I used to sing 'Coventry Carol' [to him]," his mother says. "One day I heard him, without being able to say the words, actually repeating the tune . . . and it scared the heck out of me. It's weird to hear this little song in a minor key come floating out of an infant's room. And he could keep the beat to anything that was on television. He would just sit there and tap his foot."

Top: Baby Chris. (Photograph courtesy of the Kirkpatrick family)
Bottom: Adult Chris. (Photograph by Lawrence David, copyright © 1998 by Bantam Doubleday Dell)

It wasn't until Chris was about two and a half years old that his mother started to notice his innate ability to perform. Beverly recalls, "When he was two and a half I took him to see *Man of La Mancha,* and he came home and he had memorized two of the songs. Another time we took him to a family reunion—all his [older] cousins were eight, nine, ten years old. They all performed their trios and duets on flutes and such, and when it was all over he jumped up on the place they were performing and said, 'Hey, what about me!' and he broke into song. He could sing a two-part harmony when he was two and a half."

But Chris says he didn't realize how much he enjoyed performing until he was in fifth grade, when he won the lead role in a high-school production of the musical *Oliver!* From then on, he started to take music more seriously, playing trombone in high school and studying keyboard and guitar.

While he was serious about his music, he wasn't serious about much else, says his mom. "He was funny. He had a great deal of honor and integrity and he was always really offended if anyone challenged that. I think part of the reason he was funny was because he was really, really small. Tiny, almost elflike. And he was gifted in music and language skills from the time he was really small, so he sort of stuck out. He had to go to gifted classes, and that brands you in some circles. For him to survive being small and not get beat up every day, he became the funniest person in school."

She also describes Chris as a "hardworking" kid who went out and got a job bagging groceries as soon as he was old enough."And he was high-energy," Beverly adds. "He got kicked out of piano class because he was doing really well but the piano teacher was going crazy because he couldn't sit still on the piano bench. He was up on one knee and wagging the other and almost upside down trying to play piano."

It's easy to see how he got his reputation for being the wild man of the group. His bandmates confirm that he lives up to it. "Chris is too much. He's crazy. Sometimes he's overwhelming," Justin says. Lance adds, "He just loves to have fun. Anything you can do dangerous or crazy, he'll do."

Chris laughs and agrees, "I'm the trouble. I'm the poison in the group—the troublemaker. Every day I'll do something and try to get the other guys to do it."

His mother recalls one of his countless wacky antics when he was growing up, first in Clarion, Pennsylvania, and then in Ohio. "When he was in high school he played the lieutenant who dies in *South Pacific,* and he was terribly beautiful and sort of waiflike. [He had] all the people in the audience bawling. He was the last one to come out when the play was over, and they just couldn't wait to applaud him and cry again . . . but he came out in a hula skirt and a coconut bra! He never ceased to do things like that."

Beverly says Chris lets the world see a lot of that humorous side. "The part that they don't see a lot of is that he's very, very sensitive. He cares an extraordinary amount for people. Everything matters to him so much. It's funny that people think he's so funny and everything—but at the same time I don't think they really realize the depth of him as an individual and how much he really cares for people."

In fact, Chris's compassionate side nearly won out. Before he took the plunge into a musical career, he considered becoming a psychologist. "I started my college education [majoring] in theater, but then I branched off into music and psychology." He thought of combining his interests. "There are some people who don't respond to anything but music," he explains, "and they use that as therapy." But he's glad he made the choice he did, because he couldn't picture himself doing anything else but performing. "I love the [music] business," he says.

After school Chris moved down to Orlando, where his father was living at the time, to "pursue an acting career. But then I started leaning toward music. I'd done little gigs with a friend of mine and a guitar, in coffee shops, and then I auditioned for this group called the Caroling Company. Every Christmas they contract a certain amount of carolers to go, and you're guaranteed a couple of days' work with good pay. I got the Universal gig through that."

At Universal, Chris sang with a fifties doo-wop group outside a restaurant. Mutual friends introduced him to Joey Fatone, and he was already friendly with Justin Timberlake. Soon Chris started to think about putting a group together. "I'd done some groups before," he says. "But this time I really wanted to take it seriously. I love that kind of four-part, five-part harmony, so I called up a bunch of my buddies . . ." And the rest is history.

Chris brings a wide range of musical influences to the group. His classically trained high soprano stands out in 'N Sync's harmonies, and while his mother says he "sings opera beautifully," Chris looks to artists like the Beatles, Simon and Garfunkel, Michael Jackson, Boys II Men, and Az Yet as his primary musical inspirations.

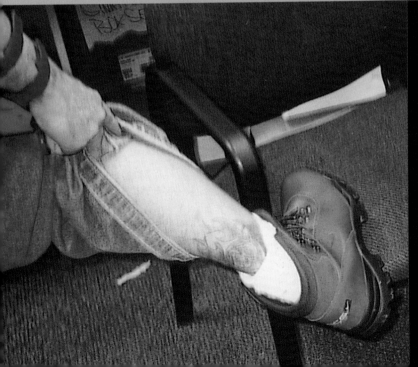

Chris delights in "all parts" of his career, especially "touring and live performances." And though "it feels really good to be coming home," to the United States after touring Europe, he considers traveling the world the best part of the job. His favorite places include South Africa, Mexico, and Spain, and he finds it fascinating how the fans abroad "respond to different songs in different places." But life on the road isn't always easy. "I miss my family and friends a lot," he confesses.

Chris also acknowledges that his life has changed since his success. "It's a lot busier. You see a lot more. You meet a lot more people. It's great because we get to present our music to a variety of different people."

Chris's mother is quick to agree that Chris's life has changed with his success. But she adamantly states that *he* hasn't. "Chris had the advantage of being pretty much grown up when this whole thing started. So, he had a good identity—he was established as who he was, and I think that's a real plus for him. Then when all the fame came along it was easy for him to handle it. Because he's real comfortable with who he is."

She adds that "he realizes more the value of friends he had before he was Chris of 'N Sync, because of hangers-on who love you just because you're Chris of 'N Sync. I think maybe he's a little more cynical about people. Other than that, he's the same person he always was."

Beverly trusts that Chris will avoid some of the pitfalls that come along with over-whelming popularity. "I wish he could fly as high as anybody can fly with what he's doing and come through it safely, and when he lands he can take off for his next adventure," she says.

While Chris's mom says she's "met a lot of really nice people, and I got to see Acapulco, and I get to hear Chris sing more often," his fame has had some ill effects on the home front. "The bad things are we have a total loss of privacy. We've had tour buses circling the block. His sister Emily, who is sixteen, is now home-schooling, and part of the reason for that is that people were starting to bother her to the point that she couldn't function in school. I have people who come and see me at work. I have people who call me at work.

People have certain expectations of what his life is like privately and what our lives are like. I had one girl come over and she said, 'I spent the whole day worrying about what to say to your maid.' And I said, 'As you can see, there is no maid in this house!' Their expectations are sometimes a little bit difficult to live with."

She adds that Chris's younger siblings "resent not having him. We've lost a lot of what we would normally have as a family. But he does manage to get home most holidays, and when he's home he spends his holidays with us. They're all just basically glad that he gets to do what he loves to do and he's actually able to make a living out of it." When he walks in the door, Beverly explains that Chris's five-year-old sister and his three nephews "totally attack him and for the next four hours he's like a jungle gym. He's a good brother. His sisters all tell him that."

Because she works full-time, gives voice lessons part-time, and helps care for her grandchildren, Beverly doesn't get to travel with Chris as often as she would like. But she is always there for him when he needs advice. "When he misses a key—I tell him. My dad was more of a perfectionist than I was and I would say, 'Your grandfather rolled over twice in his grave on that last note.' And he knows I'm the

only person in the world he can call who will give him an honest answer to 'How did I do?' I always tell him the truth about his music.

"Now, when he says, 'Do you like my hair?', then I lie. I know that with your kids if you say, 'I hate it,' that means he's going to keep it for twenty more years. So I say 'Oh, yeah, cool, I love it! I'm going to get mine done like that next week!'"

Chris is ecstatic that he has fulfilled his dream and performs for a living, and even happier that his group is a success. He even got a tattoo on his ankle of the design that adorns the CD, so that he can always remember when the album hit platinum. "I'm just happy that we're together and doing all this together," he says. "Just success for the group is what I hope for. I have a blast with these guys. They're like my brothers. Nothing better than going around the world with your brothers and best friends."

He especially enjoys studio time, and collaborating on songs. "We all have different roles [in the studio]. A lot of times a couple of us will pair off and go in and write different things. Justin and I have written a couple of raps off of our songs that we've done. And we've written some music together. JC writes a bit. When we all get a chance in the studio we like to write." One day Chris hopes to work with the likes of Busta Rhymes and Missy Elliot.

Offstage and out of the studio, Chris enjoys sports, especially football. "When we have downtime we love playing sports. I'm a big sports buff. I love football. I love basketball." He particularly enjoys cheering on the Pittsburgh Steelers or the Penn State Nittany Lions.

He goes on, "I've loved football since I was a baby. I didn't have a pacifier, I had a little football I used to suck on. I played football when I was in junior high and high school, and I adored it. It was the best experience, and you make some great friends playing football. It's fun to compete. I'm not great. I can catch a football. I can throw a football. I can kick a football. But I don't know what to judge my football talent on. Maybe in the group I'm one of the top five," he jokes.

In his scarce spare time, Chris enjoys skating, martial arts, and going to concerts. "We went to Boys II Men," he says. "And the Rolling Stones actually had a great concert ontreal."

He describes his on- and offstage looks as "exactly the same"; he prefers baggy jeans, alls, and oversized team jerseys for a comfortable yet cool look. He says that for him all the guys, styles really don't vary in and out of the spotlight. "Sometimes we could wear the clothes we have on onstage."

Though Chris says he doesn't really have a girlfriend, he explains, "I've got girls I go with. But there's nobody I can officially say is my girlfriend. The girls I go out with lly live so far away that I never get a chance to see them."

Chris's dream girl has "a very beautiful smile. Her eyes and her smile are what say it o me. Of course everyone wants to go with a great personality. Mostly someone you with. Somebody who completes your sentences." Unfortunately, while Chris remains with the group, it may be a while before he finds the perfect mate.

How does he handle the grueling schedule of a pop singer? Chris answers that he copes keeping real. You can be a nobody one day and a big star the next day and a nobody day after that," he says. It's apparent that this philosophy helps Chris keep his feet y planted on the ground.

According to his mom, Chris is still "real" and hasn't changed from the caring kid she vs and loves. "This is a good example of Chris," she says. "[When he was growing up] vere really poor, and we had only about two days of food left in our freezer, and prob- a week left until the end of the month and we got more money. Someone came to our —we lived over a store—and told us that the people who lived over another store 1 the way had had nothing to eat for that day and the day before. Chris went into the en and got half of everything we had and handed it to these people and said, 'Take it em.' That's Chris, and he hasn't changed."

Joshua "JC" Scott Chasez: Serious and Sexy

Birth date: August 8, 1976

Place of birth: Washington, D.C.

Eyes: Blue

Hair: Brown

Home: Orlando, Florida

Family: Mom, Karen; dad, Roy; sister, Heather, 20; brother, Tyler, 17

Favorite food: Chinese

Car: Jeep

Star sign: Leo

Best mates: Sagittarius, Libra, Aries, Gemini

Favorite films: All the Star Wars and Indiana Jones movies

Favorite color: Blue

Favorite music: Brian McKnight, Seal, Sting

Collector's items: Hard Rock Cafe menus

Favorite childhood toy, according to Mom: Lego, and a Raggedy Andy that his grandmother made for him

Favorite 'N Sync song: "It changes day to day."

IF YOU DARE JC CHASEZ to do something, chances are he'll do it. That's exactly how he broke into show business in the first place. "I was dared into doing a talent show," he confides. "I was over at my friend's house one day, and these girls we knew came over and asked, 'Please, we would win the talent show with you guys if you dance with us because you're such great dancers.' My friend Kacy said, 'Man, I don't know about all this stuff,' but you know girls have their way of being persuasive. So Kacy said, 'I dare you to do it,' and I said, 'I dare *you* to do it.' And so we did it, and we won first place. Even though I did it because I was dared to, I was happy that we won. We did it a couple more times, and wherever we went we won first place; we were taking all the ribbons. I just did it for kicks. After that, my mom spotted an ad in the paper for auditions for *The Mickey Mouse Club*. I just went for the heck of it. I didn't think I had a chance because I had never done anything like it before. It was my first audition, but sure enough, I scored it. I got pretty lucky."

JC's mom, Karen Chasez, remembers the dance competitions as the experience that encouraged her usually shy son to come out of his shell. "We knew he had close to perfect pitch and a wonderful soprano voice when he was twelve, but he was too shy to perform. And when he was thirteen and had done dance competitions for a little while, he got the courage to do vocals, and he walked away with first place and a lot of encouragement to proceed with that."

Top: Baby JC with Dad and dog.
Middle: The Chasez family: Roy, JC, Karen, Heather, and Tyler.
Bottom: JC at seven years old.
(Photographs courtesy of the Chasez family)

When Karen spotted the advertisement for open auditions for *The Mickey Mouse Club,* she believed JC just might have a chance. "They came to Washington, D.C., and held an open call. Five hundred kids showed up," she remembers. "At the end of that night they taped twelve; the talent scout took me aside at that point and told me that Josh had a very good chance at making the final cut, even in L.A. Disney auditioned twenty thousand kids in the United States and Canada that year. They hired ten, and he was one of them." JC has many great memories of his years on the show. "The friends I made on that show are lifetime friends. My fondest memories were hanging out at the beach, hanging at the apartment with my buddies and costars, Tony and Dale."

"I did the *Mouse Club* for four years," he continues. "After the *Mouse Club* wrapped up I moved out to L.A. for a couple of months. [I started] to learn how to write by working with different people there. From L.A. I went home for a few weeks to Maryland; then I lived in Nashville for a little while with friends. I was writing in Nashville and singing on demos—I just wanted to do the behind-the-scenes thing for a while, just to learn my craft. Because I knew the music was what I wanted to do. I didn't want to pursue the acting first off. I wanted to pursue the music end of it. At the same time I wanted to learn a little about what goes on behind the scenes. I figured the more I knew the better off I'd be." Then he landed back in Orlando, where he hung out with old *Mouse Club* buddy Justin, and Joey Fatone, who was friendly with some Mouseketeers who went to his Orlando high school.

JC's parents are thrilled that he's using the talents he took such pains to hide when he was younger. "When Josh signed up for the vocals at the dance competition, he didn't have the money, so the dance instructor said she would put up the money," JC's father, Roy, remembers. "She put up the money and she kept waiting and waiting and waiting, and she would say, 'Josh, are you ready?' And he'd say, 'Yep.' And she asked, 'Well, why don't you sing something for us?' And then he'd say, 'I'm not ready.' Finally the night before the com-

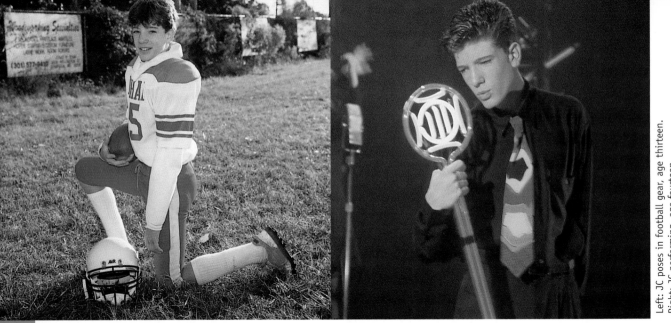

petition, she said, 'Josh, you have to show me at least that you can sing.' JC's mother, Karen, laughs as she recalls, " [The dance instructor] said, 'I paid an entrance fee, but I don't even know if he can sing!' And I said, 'He can sing all right, but I'm floored that he agreed to do it!' He'd never agreed to sing in public before." His mother remembers that fateful song—the first he ever performed for an audience." It was Richard Marx's 'Right Here Waiting for You.' "

Though his parents noticed JC's vocal ability from three years old, they "never pushed him, because he was so shy." He even stayed away from the Maryland Boys' Choir "because it was too scary for him."

It's hard to believe that this is the same lead singer who plays to the cameras with such alluring self-confidence in 'N Sync's videos. But JC claims it was more perfectionism than bashfulness that kept him from going onstage when he was younger. "It wasn't being scared to be in front of people," he asserts. "My thing was that I have to give them the best that I have. I was always afraid of things not going well. I'm still always nervous about what's going to happen onstage."

If he wasn't a born ham, a love of music was instilled in JC shortly after birth. His dad credits Karen's side of the family with cultivating a love of music in the Chasez clan. "My wife's family is very much into music. We would have gatherings where we would all sing songs. At Christmas we sing a lot of songs as we open gifts. I know that the musical aspect was there and the love of music was there."

Karen agrees. "In our household, while there are no musical performers, music has always been prized. We played a wide variety of music. The kids have an appreciation of classical music, and Josh likes jazz. And I think music has been valued in all the family settings since Josh was small. The whole environment of the family was a musical part of life, even though we weren't performers ourselves."

Both of JC's parents say that he is still "somewhat quiet and shy. He enjoys spending a lot of time by himself. He enjoys watching movies, and relaxing, and kind of kicking back."

His mother also characterizes him as "young at heart. He does a lot of playing in the yard in the neighborhood, throwing the ball in the street, practicing his handsprings in the yard—those sorts of things, even though he's in his twenties."

But even when he's home, JC doesn't stop working. "He will go through all the instruments we have here," says JC's dad, who thinks the word "gifted" best describes his son. "And he'll go around in circles with them. He'll pluck on the piano for five minutes, then go to the guitar, and he won't do it more than five to ten minutes at a time, but he's constantly playing some instrument like that all day long."

JC acknowledges that he's "always been a workaholic. Once I go into something I dive into it with both feet. When it was school, I was totally into school . . . once I pick something, I look at it and I start to get into it pretty much." Bandmate

Photograph by Lawrence David, copyright © 1998 by Bantam Doubleday Dell

Joey agrees, "He's very goal oriented. He's very focused on what he does."

JC adds, "I'm like the sanity in this big mix. Everybody's got their job . . . my job is to remind people to be on time. I'm the serious one, and I like to make sure that everything runs smooth." He continues, "I'm the guy who gets everybody to buckle down. As far as finding the focal point, that's what I do. When it's time to buckle down I say, 'This is what we need to buckle down on and why.' "

It's this kind of focus and dedication that keeps JC down-to-earth and plugging ahead. His fame isn't new-found, since he enjoyed a solid fan base from his *Mouse Club* years. But even so, he never expected his popularity to hit the heights it's at today." I don't concentrate on the fame that much," he says realistically. "I just concentrate on the task in front of me. Being famous is what it is, but that's not what I think about day to day. What I think about day to day is 'We have to get this song done, we have to get our show ready.' I don't concentrate on the fame; I concentrate on my craft."

And while he enjoys being one of the group's front-men, JC is realistic in understanding that this may not always be the case. "If I wasn't in front of everything I'd be behind the scenes," he explains. "Maybe as an engineer in the studio, or something like that, because I like the business itself. I just don't know if I'll always be the artist. I don't mind being the button pusher, the technical person,

either. I think I would be an engineer, showing people how to run the studio . . . because I like being around it."

But for the time being, he's pleased with the opportunity to use his vocal talents. "I take a piece of a lot of different styles," he says, describing his sound. "I listen to a lot of different kinds of music. I went through a bunch of different phases in my life musically. I listen to everything, and I take a little bit from each person. I like jazzy stuff and slow songs, jazzy chords. I can take some Stevie Wonder or Brian McKnight or the raspy, breathy sound of Sting or Seal, or sing real hard and belty. Different songs make me feel different ways."

He feels that it's not just *his* style that makes the group's sound so special. "The thing about us is that we're [all] so diverse. We can sing the pop stuff, we can sing R&B, we can sing rock and roll. Our strong point [is that] we come from so many different musical influences."

'N Sync's musical lexicon is so varied that JC believes if the band were to work with another artist, it could be anyone. "We could adapt to anybody, and I think anybody could adapt to us because we sing so many different styles. So we wouldn't have problems making things work." When pressed about exactly whom he would like to work with he says, "To cut a song with Janet Jackson and to dance with her would be phat."

Like his bandmates, JC loves all parts of his job. "I like it all at different times. I like going to the concerts and relaying it to the people and getting immediacy back—not listening to the radio to see how many times a day they play it. I like the immediate response. I like to see the look on people's faces when they hear that song," he says, while he adds that studio time is also up there among his favorite parts of the job. "I like being in the studio and creating something new."

He also adores the travel, something his mother says was always a passion of his. "When he was in elementary school, for three years we consecutively made family car trips west and had a lot of fun adventures just exploring the U.S. by automobile. All three children have very fond memories of that. And I know that even after traveling a good bit of the world, Josh thinks of those trips as some of his most enjoyable experiences," Karen Chasez says. "We hit thirty-eight states in three years. It broadened their perspective and gave them a sense of the world being a lot bigger than your own little neighborhood."

When JC travels, he likes to add to his thirty-strong Hard Rock Cafe menu collection. His most prized items hail from Malaysia, Japan, Paris, and London. But the *pièce de résistance* was "a pin of a menu that I snagged in London. A lady was waiting on me and she was wearing a pin of a menu," he explains. "There's only fifteen to twenty given out every year. And it's only for employees who do exceptional work around the *world*. I gave her my whole spiel . . . she says, 'Let me talk to my boss.' She's not really supposed to do that. The next thing you know, she pleads with her boss, and she comes back and says, 'We'll get them to make another to send to us . . . have this one.' "

JC also digs the diversity of the audiences 'N Sync travels to. "I like seeing the different cultures and seeing the way people carry on day to day," he comments. "I like the people. I like seeing how people live their lives—that's what's interesting to me. You can go all around the world and people do things a little differently. We're still very much the same because we're all human beings, but we're different because we've been taught different ways. It's fascinating to see how an entire country thinks one way, and our entire country thinks another way, and they handle situations differently. It's neat."

But the best times are when his family comes along on the road, JC says. "My brother comes on tour with me, more than anybody, because he's young and still in school and we get along really well. My parents come out on tour too; they all do at different times."

Left: Photograph courtesy of Kaja Gula. Right: Photograph copyright © 1998 by Max Goldstein/Star File

JC sees mostly pluses in his skyrocketing career, but he does admit that he wishes he had a less hectic schedule and "more time to myself." In the little spare time he has, he mostly likes to sleep. He also enjoys going to the movies, "because when I'm at a movie, it's nice to be taken out of reality for two hours. It's a runaway," he explains.

He describes his personal style as "changing day to day. Some days I'll be conservative. Other days, laid-back. But I don't dress crazy. [My style] ranges from semiconservative to funky."

JC woefully declares that he never has the time to date. One day, though, he hopes to meet someone who is "fun, because I work all the time. I need someone who's going to show me a good time, because I'm always so focused. I need somebody who brings a little fun out of me—somebody who makes me laugh. And somebody who will make me want to do things for her." His idea of a great date? "Going to the theater to see a live play—but not a musical."

JC says he likes to spend a lot of his downtime with his family. He describes them as "very supportive of what I do." So supportive were they that when he was working on *The Mickey Mouse Club* his parents ran two separate households to keep the family together. Karen stayed at the family home outside Washington, D.C., while Roy headed up the

Orlando house. "The children were back and forth depending on summer and school time," Karen says. "There've been pros and cons—it's not always easy. I think our children would have liked to have a little less of a hectic schedule and both Mom and Dad. But the plus side has been that the travel has been something all of us enjoy."

Luckily, the Chasezes have been able to keep their home "out of the spotlight" and don't have fans invading their privacy as do some of the other boys' families. But Karen says she enjoys watching fans react to her son's performances. "It's fun to see him do a concert and see everybody singing and having a good time. It's great to see [the fans] be thrilled to get an autograph or posing for a picture. He's doing something he loves, and the fans are having a great time. We really don't spend a lot of the time thinking about the famous part."

And while JC's dad shares some common worries of showbiz parents, such as "people making bad decisions for Josh" and "people with ulterior motives using him," he still delights in watching his son do his thing. "That's Josh, he's doing his job, and it so happens that his job is making a lot of people happy with his music."

Like most proud parents, JC's mother and father are happy about his success. His mother says, "We think it's wonderful that he has a chance to do something that he truly enjoys, and that he's good at, and he can make it the focus of his professional life. I think it's the thing that most of us hope for ourselves, that we will be able to find a niche to really contribute, do a good job, and we love it, and it also is our work. There are many, many people who don't have that privilege, and he's aware that it is a privilege."

JC does feel lucky to have made it in the music world. "We know there's a million other groups out there doing this," he says. "We want to be one of the few that are around for a long time. We feel like the only way to do that is to be ourselves. Because people will see through an act. They will see through the phoniness. But if they see something genuine, and they see something real, and if we respect people the way we were raised to respect people, we should have no problem."

Justin Randall Timberlake:Southern Heart and Soul

Birth date: January 31, 1981

Place of birth: Memphis, Tennessee

Eyes: Blue

Hair: Blond

Home: Orlando, Florida

Family: Parents and stepparents, Lynn and Paul Harless and Lisa and Randy Timberlake; brothers, Jonathan, 5, and Steven, 5 months

Favorite foods: Cereal, pasta

Car: Mercedes M Class

Star sign: Aquarius

Best mates: Libra, Sagittarius, Aries, Gemini

Favorite films: *The Usual Suspects, Twelve Monkeys*

Favorite color: Baby blue

Favorite music: hip-hop

Favorite TV show: *Seinfeld*

Collector's items: Sneakers, basketball gear

Favorite childhood toy, according to Mom: "Different guitars. He always dragged around some kind of little plastic banjo or guitar."

Favorite 'N Sync song: " 'God Must Have Spent a Little More Time on You' because it is *the* perfect love song. I'm a very spiritual person so it relates to me."

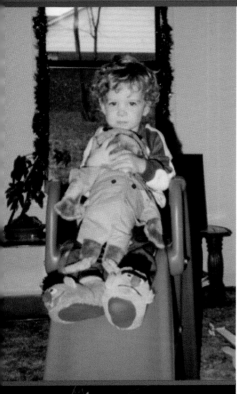

THOUGH HE'S ONLY IN HIS TEENS, Justin Timberlake always knew one day he'd have a musical career. "I pretty much popped out singing," he says.

"Justin has always, always exhibited great talent for music," his mother, Lynn Harless, confirms. "From when he was a tiny baby, not walking or talking yet, when he was three to four months old, you could turn music on and he would always keep time with the music, kicking to the beat of the music. We would laugh about it . . . we'd put slow music on, then fast music. He was like a little toy!"

"From the time he could talk he was singing right away," she continues. "His father has a really beautiful voice—he was in a group, a bluegrass band, when Justin was very small, so he grew up listening to people harmonizing around him all the time. I think Justin was about two and a half years old and we were coming home from a bluegrass festival; he started singing harmony with the radio. The music was always in his head, he could always hear the harmony parts. Some people you have to teach to hear those things and some people have a God-given talent for it. It was just always there with him."

Justin is the show-business veteran of 'N Sync, even though he's the youngest in the group. "I've pretty much always been in entertainment. I did *The Mickey Mouse Club* for two years and before that I did *Star Search* when I was about ten or eleven. Before that I was singing in church and playing basketball in school. That's really all I did, besides

Top: Young Justin.
Bottom: Justin at age five. (Photographs courtesy of Paul and Lynn Harless)

Left: Copyright © 1998 by Anthony Cutajar/London Features. Right: Photograph courtesy of Kaja Gula

school. But," he admits, "I never imagined something like this where we tour the world. Where you never, ever have free time."

Justin considers that his primary vocal roots are in the church. "I come from a big background of family singers, singing in church. My grandmother, my daddy, my uncles, my aunts, I got it from them."

His first taste of stardom came in the fourth grade, and it would foreshadow his future as a singing, dancing sex symbol. His mother remembers this turning point for Justin: "When he was in fourth grade he and his friends got a New Kids on the Block lip-sync act together. They went to a little talent thing at school, and he actually sang one of the songs—'I'll Be Loving You Forever.' Somebody saw them and asked them to come entertain at another school. One of the other little boys in the group—his aunt owned a limo—sent a limo to pick them up. They dressed up like New Kids on the Block and went to this other school and entertained. When they ran offstage all these little girls chased them down the hall! A teacher had to barricade them in a room, and these little girls were standing in the hall and chanting their names!"

That experience encouraged Justin to enter some amateur contests. Then, a little less than a year later, Lynn says proudly, "*Star Search* came and did a big talent search in Memphis and he was one of the people who was chosen to go on the show. He sang a country-and-western song, and he was only eleven years old." That small step would lead to an even larger gig for Justin. "It so happened that *Star Search* was filmed [in Orlando] on the soundstage next to *The Mickey Mouse Club*. Justin always used to watch it on TV—and we found out when we were there that they were holding auditions for new cast members, and they would be holding an open audition in Nashville. We flew home from *Star Search* and went to the audition, and they chose him to be on the show. They auditioned thirty thousand kids and they hired seven that year."

Justin spent two years on *The Mickey Mouse Club,* where he became fast friends with JC Chasez. "It was a great experience all around," Justin says. "The whole thing was amazing for me."

Besides singing, young Justin loved dancing and playing basketball, and he looked up to Michael Jackson and Michael Jordan. His mother describes him as "a real private kind of person. Even when he was a very small child he would go into his room and play by himself for hours and hours. He values his quiet time; he's somebody that needs a lot of quiet time. He's very thoughtful about things. He reflects on the things that happen to him—he analyzes everything. He still spends a lot of time by himself when he's at home. He's a really quiet kind of guy."

Lynn continues that she thinks Justin's early introduction to fame and showbiz has had a positive effect on him. "I feel like he's grown a lot from it," she asserts. "I don't think it's changed him as a person. I think he's had a lot of positive changes, I don't think any negative changes. He's only seventeen so he's growing up extremely fast. I stopped traveling with them a year ago . . . so he's traveled pretty much on his own with the other

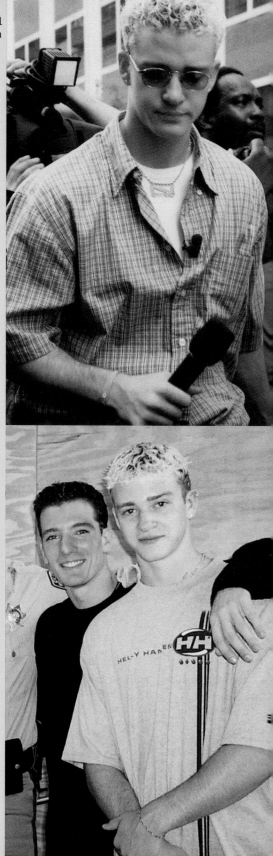

guys for the last year. He's always been a really good kid, he's never been any trouble, and he's always been really, really serious about his singing. He's grown a lot—he's matured way beyond his years, and of course I feel that's from all the experiences he's had in the entertainment business."

The guys in 'N Sync hold a special place in their hearts for Lynn, who was very involved in the group's early days. "I spent the first year and a half on the road with the boys," she says fondly. "Justin was young when they started 'N Sync—he was only fourteen. Of course, he was too young to be by himself and since I had to be there anyway, and since we developed the group ourselves, that was something I took part in, and that was the greatest experience for me."

"She did a lot of our managerial work," adds Chris, who with JC shared a home with Lynn and Justin until spring of 1998. In fact, the experience she received from helping the boys led Lynn to fulfill a lifelong dream and open her own management company. She currently handles the up-and-coming girl group Innosense, but 'N Sync will always be Lynn's first baby. "I love all the guys so much," she says. "The comment that [I] get about the guys the most is that they are so down-to-earth, so easy to work with, they're all so cooperative. That's the thing people still say about them, that they haven't changed . . . and they'll have a long-term success because they are so close to each other and they haven't let this go to their heads. They're just having a ball doing what they love to do. They're just so excited that they can have a life doing what they want to do."

With her love of the music business, it's no wonder that Lynn is extremely supportive of her son's career choice. But that doesn't mean she doesn't worry the way other moms do. "The only negative thing I can think of from doing the kind of thing he does is the lack of contact with your family and friends—especially for somebody Justin's age," she confides. "I think it's really, really hard. He calls us a lot. That's the time that as a mother I worry, when he calls me and I can hear that's he's lonely or stressed or fatigued. They work so hard—they work such long hours. It's a hard, hard job. Sometimes I ask him, 'Are you happy? You don't have to do this—you can just go back to school.' His response is always, 'I could never *not* do this. I'm just tired. I just miss my family.' So when he gets a little homesick that's hard for me. I just want him to be happy, and I know that there's nothing else in his life that he could ever do that would make him as happy as music. I just want him to be very well rounded and have a lot of positive experiences—grow as much as he can possibly grow and just to be happy."

It's clear that Justin is committed to his career. "All my friends back home always tell me how lucky I am to be doing something like this," he says. "And sometimes I'll want to go back and play basketball for my old school or something and then I think about how much I love doing this and how if I got away from this, how unhappy I would be. I think everybody makes sacrifices to do the things they want to do."

"Because that's what I wanted to do," he goes on. "I always said it's what I wanted to do. And my mom would say, 'If at any time you don't want to do this, just let me know. I don't want you to feel pressured that you have to do it.' A lot of kids get into show business and they feel a lot of pressure. I mean it is a lot of pressure, but this is what I wanted."

When Justin is on the road they keep in touch via cell phone. "We all have cell phones—our telephone bills are astronomical," his mother says. "Wherever we are in the

Photograph courtesy of Kaja Gula

world we talk to each other every day. Our family requires contact, and we decided we would do this as long as it didn't have a detrimental effect on the family."

But his mother says that while Justin's fame is hard "because we spend so much time apart," it's had many positive effects on the family. "It's opened a lot of doors for us, and given us the opportunity to see Justin be successful at something he really loves. It's brought us closer as a family. Although we don't get to spend as much time together, virtually all of our time is high-quality time. And our family is really, really close because of that. We value our time together so much. I think a lot of kids don't value family time, but Justin knows what it means to come home and how important home is."

Justin loves what he does despite the long hours and separation from his family. He especially enjoys "touring, and making new songs from scratch. [But] the biggest gratification to me is being on tour. When you can just stop singing and hold the mike into the audience, and they're singing for you, it's the biggest gratification for me."

Though Justin is the youngest of the guys, they don't treat him like a baby brother. "It's not really like baby, daddy, oldest, youngest," he explains. "We all consider ourselves equal. I think it pays off; we all respect each other. That's something that pays off when you tour with each other because we're together all the time."

His cohorts have a tremendous amount of respect for Justin. "Justin is the all-around guy. He's good at everything he does," Lance says. As a lead singer in the group, Justin has a distinctive soulful voice that blends perfectly with the harmonies of the other guys. Vocally, Justin looks up to Brian McKnight, and he claims he would love to work with him one day, in addition to others like Jermaine Dupri and Stevie Wonder.

Justin claims that if he wasn't in the entertainment business, he'd be playing basketball. "That's the other dream I have," he discloses. "But I'm not growing too much lately." His love of basketball is apparent in his personal style, which Justin describes as "athletic, hip-hop. I love basketball gear."

He plays as much as he can in his spare time—when he has spare time. Otherwise, he likes to "just chill" or spend time with his younger brothers. "Jonathan, the five-year-old, comes [to shows] as much as he can. He loves 'N Sync. He does his own little concerts at the house." Justin laughs. "[If we were like] Menudo, they could drop him in there as soon as I get too old to dance!"

Justin jokes, "I have twenty thousand girlfriends . . . all over the world," though that figure probably doesn't come close to the actual number of his admirers. But he seriously adds, "I don't have anybody that I come home to, no."

The girl he hopes to come home to one day must have "confidence. It always attracts me. The way she presents herself, if she's confident in herself and not insecure. On the other hand, it has to be within a certain limit. She can't be too cocky. She also must have a sense of humor. I like somebody who likes to have fun. I'm a hopeless romantic, but I don't like to be boring all the time, like 'Let's just go out to dinner.' I like to do fun stuff. I like to do things out of the blue, like 'Hey, let's go bungee jumping.' or 'Hey, let's go rock climbing.' I like to be spontaneous."

Justin treasures having a date with thousands of fans every night on tour. "We love it. We enjoy every minute of it. We love our fans. [It's] always exciting. It pumps you up. The louder they are . . . the more into it they are, the more you get pumped up."

As a private person, however, Justin regrets that he doesn't have time for himself. "As soon as you get that free time, and you want to go out, you can't," he laments. "When you want to go to the movies or something, someone will recognize you and all of a sudden it's a mob scene at the theater."

But Justin is just as quick to praise his fans. "Thank you for everything. We wouldn't be here if it wasn't for you," he says sincerely. "God bless you, you've been the reason we've made it this far, and hopefully we can keep pleasing you."

'N the Mix: A Day in the Lives of 'N Sync

MANY FANS DON'T REALIZE how much hard work each day is for the fabulous five. Here's an idea of a typical day in the busy lives of 'N Sync. The guys' schedule is completely exhausting, but they take it in stride and with a smile.

1 A.M.

The members of 'N Sync fly into New York from Atlanta after an appearance at Macy's in the southern city. They check into their midtown hotel and crash. Tomorrow they'll be up early.

5 A.M.

After only four hours' sleep, the boys wake and prepare for a grueling eighteen-hour day.

6:15 A.M.

Fresh-faced and ready to take on the world, JC, Joey, Chris, Justin, and Lance gather in their hotel lobby to meet with record company representatives and go over the day's plans. Joey sports jeans, a baby-blue button-down shirt, and his favorite Superman necklace. Lance looks well rested in his long-sleeved white thermal shirt and green cargo pants with zippers; Chris shows off his new brown and platinum dreads and is the picture of low-maintenance comfort in jeans and a white T-shirt. His silver beads dress up his look. JC wears khakis and a bright red shirt, open to show his trademark white undershirt. Justin appears laid-back in a checked shirt, jeans, and his brand-new shades.

The boys are quickly briefed on what the day holds. First they're going to ride a double-decker bus around Manhattan with Virgin founder Richard Branson to promote the opening of his new Virgin Megastore downtown.

6:30 A.M.

As soon as the guys exit the hotel, they're met by tenacious fans. The guys are happy to sign autographs and pose for pictures, despite the early hour.

6:40 A.M.

A limousine whisks the guys downtown so they can board the Virgin Megabus.

7 A.M.

'N Sync arrives at the new Virgin Megastore in Union Square. Already fans are lined up around the block to catch a glimpse of their favorite group.

7:15 A.M.

The guys are incredibly chipper as they climb onto the double-decker bus. Even though it's seventy-nine degrees at this early hour, Chris thinks it's cold compared to Orlando. Richard Branson boards the bus with Petula Clark, singer of the sixties hit "Downtown." Richard and Petula introduce themselves to the guys. Immediately they're all fast friends.

7:30 A.M.

'N Sync and Petula Clark practice harmonies. 'N Sync learn the words to "Downtown"; Petula learns "I Want You Back" and "Tearin' Up My Heart." Richard Branson declares himself a sixth member of the group, joking that he can't sing but can offer the guys more good looks.

8 A.M.

The bus takes off for the morning tour of Manhattan. First stop, Times Square. Frenzied fans await as the bus pulls into the early-morning glitter of New York's neon hub. Lucky fans who know the words to "Downtown" get to board the bus and meet the guys. Afterward, 'N Sync gives away T-shirts and signs autographs for the crowd. Then the guys break into a rendition of "Downtown" with Petula, and Petula joins 'N Sync for "I Want You Back" while the crowd sings along.

8:30 A.M.

The bus pulls away and weaves its way through midtown, sailing by Rockefeller Center, *The Today Show,* and Grand Central Terminal, as the guys sing "Tearin' Up My Heart" for morning commuters. People on the street point, wave, and boogie to the beat.

9 A.M.

The bus pulls to a stop in front of the New York Public Library, where the guys rouse the crowd with "I Want You Back." Richard Branson climbs aboard one of the library's famous stone lions as fans crowd the stairs. More lucky fans get to board the bus. The boys are having a great time, seeing the sights of New York and meeting their fans.

9:30 A.M..

The bus travels down to Greenwich Village, with fans in hot pursuit. The boys joke about the traffic lights and low tree branches in the winding Village streets. "Duck! Traffic light!" the guys call, making sure they don't get knocked off the open top deck of the bus.

10 A.M.

The bus continues downtown, through the West Village and onto the West Side Highway. The boys perform an a cappella version of the classic "The Lion Sleeps Tonight" for workers at the World Trade Center. The boys call out, flirting with some of the nicely dressed businesswomen on the streets. Chris jokes around, doing his best "Cartman" from *South Park* into the mike.

Photographs by Lawrence David, copyright © 1998 by Bantam Doubleday Dell

10:30 A.M.

The bus returns to Union Square. As they approach, the 'N Sync guys sing "Here We Go." The number of fans surrounding the block has multiplied to a staggering crowd. They chant "'N Sync has got the flow!" along with the music. Then it seems as if a thousand girls wave and scream as the guys perform "I Want You Back" one more time.

11 A.M.

The guys return to the hotel for a quick lunch and some chill time to recover from the morning excitement.

1 P.M.

The band waits in the dressing room at the Virgin Megastore at Union Square. Three thousand excited fans mob the store; many of them have been waiting since seven in the morning. Their piercing screams echo throughout the huge space, and excitement builds as they wait for their idols to appear. The album *'N Sync* booms from the sound system. A chorus of fans' voices sings along, not missing a word.

1:30 P.M.

The screams suddenly get louder as Joey, Justin, JC, Lance, and Chris exit the dressing room. Security buckles up, keeping the hysterical fans from charging the stage. The guys each take a turn saying hello into their mikes. Then they sit and greet each fan as they sign CDs. Some fans present them with roses. Others give the boys stuffed animals. Many leave letters, cards, and gifts with their heroes. The guys sincerely thank each and every fan who comes to the table.

3 P.M.

Backstage, the guys open their gifts from fans. They pass around the letters and poems, which JC especially enjoys. "I enjoy the creativity, and they're interesting," he says. Chris

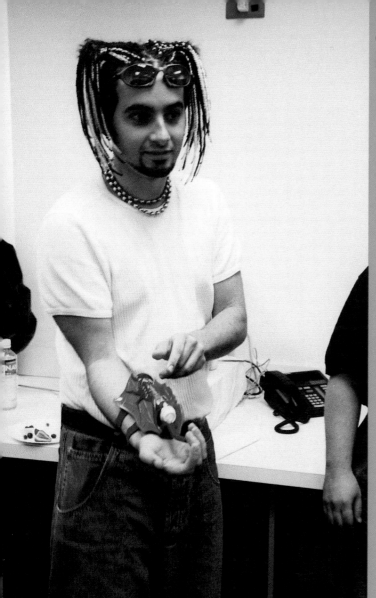

Chris plays with a gift from a fan.
(Photograph by Lawrence David, copyright © 1998
by Bantam Doubleday Dell)

is ecstatic about a Spider-man web-shooter a fan gave him, and he's webbing everyone in the room. Lance cuddles a stuffed Dalmatian, while Joey unwraps flowers. Justin can't get over the homemade cards, filled with photos and drawings.

3:30 P.M.

The boys go back to their hotel to freshen up before their next appointment. Miraculously, they don't seem to be losing a bit of steam.

4 P.M.

The guys head over to MTV to tape the show *Artist's Cut*. They're taped one at a time while the others hang in the green room. As they watch videos and munch on a cheese platter, the guys study the moves of the likes of Missy Elliot and Will Smith.

5 P.M.

It seems that JC wins out. When the taping is over, the guys head down to Chinatown for dinner. (JC is a Chinese-food freak.) The guys dig into plates of lo mein, sweet and sour chicken, Szechuan beef, hot-and-sour soup, and fried rice. Being on the go all day works up an appetite!

7 P.M.

The boys are energized now that their stomachs are full. A limo takes them directly to a radio station, where they do interviews for local and syndicated shows.

9 P.M.

The guys return to the hotel and rehearse for their next video. They have a two-hour work-out, getting each dance move down perfectly.

11 P.M.

After their eighteen-hour day, the guys are pooped. They hit the sack. An early rehearsal, a Macy's appearance, and a seven-hour recording session await them the next day!

JC takes a short rest before taping his segment for MTV. (Photograph by Lawrence David, copyright © 1998 by Bantam Doubleday Dell)

Out of Sync: Their Most Embarrassing Moments

EVEN WHEN YOU'RE AN INTERNATIONALLY famous singing superstar, some days are better than others. Chris, Joey, Lance, Justin, and JC will tell you that there's nothing more humbling than those *off* days. Here the guys share their most embarrassing moments—on- and offstage.

JC

Onstage: "Once we were doing a show in Switzerland, and it was the last day of the tour and everything was chaotic. My fly broke, it was wide open, and all you could see were my whities. And I didn't know because I was concentrating on the song, and it was wide open for two songs. Finally, somebody in the band told me it was broken, and I looked down and it was split wide open. So I ran backstage, and they didn't have a spare pair of pants. We were just starting a song we do where the band and us trade places, and we play the instruments and the band sings the song . . . kind of as a practical joke on the audience. So I covered my lower half with the bass guitar. After that I ran backstage and they pinned my fly shut. But it was embarrassing to have my fly wide open for two whole songs and nobody bothered to tell me."

Offstage: "My first time going skiing I knocked down a rack of skis and crashed into a cabin at the bottom of the hill, where the lifts are. They were having a ski competition that day. So I crashed in front of all the pros, knocked over everything. That was pretty dumb."

'N Sync celebrates Chris's birthday in October 1996. (Photograph courtesy of the Bass family)

Lance

Onstage: "Over in Germany we did a TV awards show. We all had to stand backstage getting ready to go on for the finale, and all go out and show our awards and wave good-bye to the camera. When the music started, someone told me to go. So I ran out on stage, but what happened was the last band hadn't gone on yet. The last group was onstage. I was out there with them and I just made a fool out of myself. Of course I was in black patent leather and they were all in yellow, so I totally stood out."

Offstage: "I fought a bull in Mexico. I thought it was a joke. They had five volunteers, four guys over forty, and me. They let this bull loose, and the first four guys got trampled. Then they put me out there with a little red cape, and it came charging at me. Charged me like six times. It hurt a lot. I made a fool out of myself in front of many people—a full stadium—who knew who I was."

Joey

Onstage: "One time I sprained my ankle [during a show] and it was so bad that my toes started to turn black and blue. And I had to do three shows, one after another. I went hopping onstage, and I was still dancing."

Offstage: "I was with the guys in Germany. I was messing around, there were some fans around. I was jumping around and I went to go kick over JC's head, and my foot was almost going to kick him in the head, so I tried to raise it a little bit higher and my other foot came out under me. I fell on my butt right in front of everybody. People pointed and poked fun at me."

Chris

Onstage: "One time we were doing one of the back flips that we do. Joey threw me over backwards, my foot slipped out, and I didn't go very good. He turned my ankle and I did a back slam. That hurt."

The group hangs out with its security personnel. (Photograph courtesy of Kaja Gula)

'N Sync with Will Smith. (Photograph courtesy of Roger Widynowski)

Offstage: "We were at the airport and my leg fell asleep. When I went to get up and take a step [my leg] wouldn't go, so I fell right there in the middle of the airport."
Justin

Onstage: "I ran onstage after a quick change with my fly unzipped. My pants almost fell down all the way to my ankles. They fell down on my thighs almost to my knees, and I grabbed them. Luckily I had a baggy basketball shirt on over them, so you couldn't see that they fell down. I also broke my thumb onstage before. It was an open-air festival in Germany; it was outside and it was really hot and they were spraying the kids with water, with this big hose, and they got some water on the stage. There's a move where we slide across the floor in one of our songs, and I slid on the water and my feet came out from under me. My first reaction was to throw my hands down—try to catch myself—and my thumb broke. Luckily it was the last song of our set. I just held the mike in my left hand the whole time."

Offstage: "It's hard to pick just one. I do something embarrassing every day."

'Nstant Hits: The Music, the Videos, the Stage Show

IT SEEMS THAT 'N SYNC'S history is repeating itself in the United States after the band's worldwide success. The same singles that topped the European charts, "I Want You Back" and "Tearin' Up My Heart," are tearing up the charts in the guys' homeland, while the debut album sits firmly in the top five, with *Home for Christmas* close behind.

'N Sync celebrates diverse musical styles on its albums, showing the many sides of the group, from hard-driven dance beats and slow, smooth ballads to a cappella and doo-wop harmonies.

While the Europeans may have been the first to get a taste of 'N Sync's style, the American audience is lucky enough to enjoy their hits—at home and abroad—along with several previously unreleased tracks. "I Just Want to Be with You," "God Must Have Spent a Little More Time on You," and "I Drive Myself Crazy" appear for the first time on the American debut.

The remake of Bread's seventies classic "Everything I Own" is also only on the American album. Audiences may recognize another cover, "Sailing," a number-one hit in 1980, when it was written and performed by Christopher Cross. 'N Sync layered the atmospheric tune with beautiful harmonies, giving it a sound that's all the guys' own. "Our manager had the idea for 'Sailing,'" Joey says. "We liked the idea. We did it and it came out really well. The other remake, 'Everything I Own,' came to us through a group called Full Force. They came up and asked us about it—what we thought about recording it."

Perhaps the only thing better than listening to the guys is watching them. On their videos and live shows, the five guys who are 'N Sync prove they're more than just a bunch of pretty faces and voices; they can move better than any boy group around.

The videos take typically one or two days—long days—to shoot. "I Want You Back" features the guys bopping to the beat in a New York street. But though the scene may look like Times Square, the guys were actually on an Orlando soundstage. "I Want You Back" was a full one-day shoot. "We shot from seven A.M. to seven A.M. the next morning," Joey says. "Then we had to do a photo shoot after that!" When the video was complete, the guys felt it lacked something: Their personalities didn't seem to come through. The boys went in

Photograph courtesy of Kaja Gula

front of the camera again, shooting snippets of an 'N Sync basketball game. Now fans can see the slick, choreographed moves of the guys onstage *and* on the courts.

"Tearin' Up My Heart" is more straightforward. It was shot in a studio, presenting the guys dancing, singing, and goofing around. But even though it looks simple, "Tearin'" took two full days to shoot. "The schedule gets hard sometimes," Justin says. "But making a video was pretty much how I expected it to be because of all the camera experience I had in *Mickey Mouse Club*. There's a lot of things that directors or producers might do that I learn every time we do a video, for lighting effects or visual effects that are just really brilliant."

If the guys look as if they're having fun in the video "For the Girl Who Has Everything," it's because they are. "For the Girl" was shot in Los Angeles on the beach, and the guys enjoyed making a video with a story line. 'N Sync, shipwrecked on a beach, find a treasure chest. As the guys croon "For the girl who has everything, I bring you love," hearts melt all over the world. Imagine getting a message in a bottle from these guys! The girl in the video truly does have everything.

Though the five had a great time frolicking in the sun and surf, there was one near-casualty. "I almost drowned," Chris says. "There was a scene where we were supposed to run around this rock. A wave hit the rock, came up over it, and took me out. I totally lost my balance. That was definitely a near-drowning."

While the videos are amazing to watch, fans have to admit that there's nothing more electric than seeing 'N Sync live. The high-energy show has plenty of dancing, not to mention their dynamic vocals. How do the guys do it? They have incredible stamina. Most of the guys say they don't even work out to keep fit, though Justin drops for 150 to 200 push-ups a day. "Just the rehearsals and the show itself keeps us in shape," Joey explains. "It's pretty demanding."

"For the most part we have a choreographer," he continues, though he adds that the guys will come up with a lot of moves on their own. "We've had three, who have been delightful to work with. They are very open-minded to our suggestions. If we don't like something, we'll change it. A lot of them have worked on videos with Usher, and Michael and Janet [Jackson]."

Though the guys are modest about their feats, a day on the road is truly draining. If a distance is more than 800 miles, they fly. But mostly they travel by bus. "The bus is our home away from home," says Lance. "It becomes so comfortable to us. When we first got on the bus it was kind of hard to adjust to that kind of life, but when you have your own bunk, that puts me to sleep. Now if I'm on something that moves, it puts me right to sleep."

A bus certainly can't compare to the guys' homes, but they make it as comfortable as they can. Their huge bus features twelve bunks for the guys and the band; two lounges, equipped with a TV, VCR, and stereo; and a kitchen. The boys like to keep a lot of candy on board, along with their favorite movies, CDs, and gifts from fans.

They've recently started to bring a furry friend on tour with them. Their dog, which they adopted from an Orlando shelter, brings hours of joy and relaxation to everyone on

the tour. At the end of the tour, they'll give the pet to a caring fan. They plan to do this on every tour from now on, so they can save as many animals as possible.

When 'N Sync arrives at a destination, the boys typically rise in the wee hours of the morning to rehearse, visit radio stations, or do in-store signings or photo shoots. That's *before* the concert. When it comes close to showtime, the guys do a sound check at the venue, and they work out any kinks they might have in their routines or go over last-minute details with the band. "We have the best band ever," Lance declares. "They were put together by a collaboration of us and the management. We had auditions, but a lot of people we just knew as friends. What came together was incredible; they all just clicked."

It takes the guys from thirty to forty-five minutes to put on makeup and dress. "We have a wardrobe person that goes on tour," Joey explains. "But they only go and get the clothes ready. We've gone out a lot of times, and literally went and got the clothes. So whatever you see is pretty much us—stuff that we like to wear."

After the clothes and makeup are ready, the guys take about half an hour for quiet time, so they can cool down from the active day and focus on the show that night. Then they carry out two preshow rituals. One is playing Hacky Sack to rev up. The other is getting together with security and the road crew to say a prayer and share a hug.

When the performance is over, the guys do a "quick out," which means they pile onto the bus the minute the show is over. There's no lingering in the dressing room, no partying backstage. They immediately get on the bus, change, snack on pizza or chicken, and start rolling toward the next destination. Their tour manager, Ibrahim Duarte, explains that this is "so no one gets hurt. If you wait too long, the fans surround the bus, and someone can get hurt."

If you haven't caught the boys on the road yet, you'll have plenty of opportunity. 'N Sync will be touring the United States for the rest of 1998 and the better part of 1999, until the next album comes out. Don't miss them—it's a one-of-a-kind concert experience you'll never forget!

Stay 'N Touch

You've heard their songs. You've seen the videos. Maybe you've been lucky enough to catch a concert. The five talented voices and faces behind 'N Sync want you to know that what you see is what you get. They're a great bunch of guys who love what they do and love to please their fans. And they'd love to hear from you!

Write to them at:

'N Sync

P.O. Box 692109

Orlando, FL 32869-2109

Or visit them on the Web at www.nsync.com

Don't miss . . .

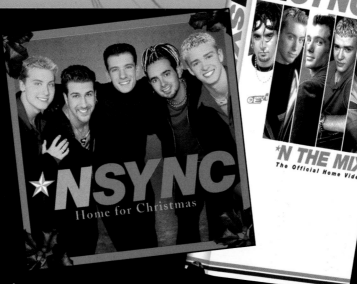

★NSYNC
M E R C H A N D I S E

WORLD TOUR CD PHOTO / WORLD TOUR '98
(black tee; size M-L only)
NSTOO1 $15.00

1999 NSYNC calendar-NSB001 $12.95

LOGO GROUP/ITINERARY
(white tee; size M-XL only)
NST002 $15.00

FLAME LOGO baseball cap
(osfa)-NSC001 $18.00

★NSYNC MERCHANDISE ORDER FORM

NAME

STREET

CITY   STATE

ZIP/POSTAL CODE COUNTRY

PHONE

IF PAYING BY CREDIT

ACCOUNT NUMBER EXP DATE

SIGNATURE

Item #	Description	Size	Price	QTY	Amount
1)					
2)					
3)					
4)					

Shipping and

Order Total	United States		International
	2nd day	Overnight	
$1-$39.99	$6.95	$12.95	$16.95
$40 -$99.99	$9.95	$15.95	$21.95
$100 and up	$15.95	$21.95	$26.95

Please allow up to two business days to process orders before shipping
Most orders will ship on the next business day.

Subtotal 1

Shippin

Subtotal 2

Tax
8.5% California
Residents Only

TOTAL

To order by mail: Complete order form and mail in with a check, money order or credit card info to:
NSYNC Merchandise, P.O. Box 883848, San Francisco, CA 94188. Please supply all information requested on the order form including a day phone #. Make checks payable to **Fan Asylum**. All amounts listed are in U.S. Dollars and need to be paid in U.S. Dollars. Send Cash at your own risk.

To order by phone: Call (415) 575-6644 Mon-Fri 9:00am - 4:30pm Pacific Time and use your MasterCard, Visa, American Express and Discover.

Shipping: You MUST add shipping and handling charges to merchandise. Please include a street address for traceable delivery. Items sent to APO, FPO, Alaska, Hawaii and P.O. Box addresses are not traceable and we do not take responsibility for lost packages.Orders will be shipped when all merchandise ordered is in stock. If an item is out of stock, this could delay your shipment.

Order by phone:
Call (415) 575-6644